YO-AET-909

INSECTS

INSECTS

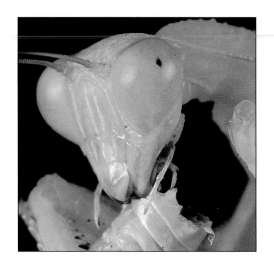

CHARTWELL
BOOKS, INC.

Published by Chartwell Books
A Division of Book Sales Inc.
114 Northfield Avenue
Edison, New Jersey 08837
USA

Copyright ©1999 Quantum Books Ltd

ISBN 0-7858-0983-X

This book is produced by
Quantum Books Ltd
6 Blundell Street
London N7 9BH

Project Manager: Rebecca Kingsley
Project Editor: Judith Millidge
Design/Editorial: David Manson
Andy McColm, Maggie Manson

The material in this publication previously appeared in
*The Practical Entomologist, Bugs, Beetles and other
Insects, Encyclopedia of Butterflies, Exotic Pet Survival
Guide*

QUMFSIT
Set in Futura
Reproduced in Singapore by Eray Scan
Printed in Singapore by Star Standard Industries (Pte) Ltd

Contents

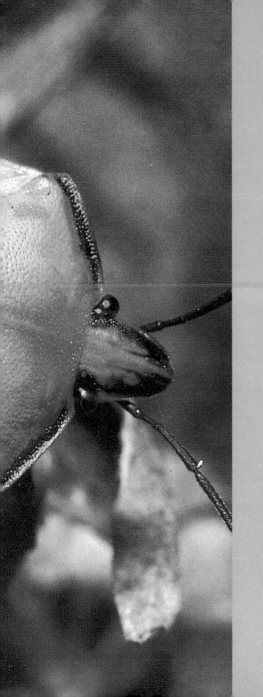

INCREDIBLE INSECTS

A reasonably strong argument can be made for saying that insects, not mammals, are the dominant life form on earth. Consider that the number of insect species is greater than the number of all other species of organisms combined; beetle species alone outnumber all plant species in the world. Despite their noticeable absence in marine environments, insects inhabit every other conceivable habitat in the world, sometimes in mind-boggling densities.

Insect Identifiers

Often any small creature with more than four legs is indiscriminately labelled a 'bug'. However, many of these creatures are not insects at all, but may belong to one of several related but very different groups.

INSECT CHARACTERISTICS

Insects have several recognizable traits that set them apart from other groups of organisms. Like other members of the Phylum Arthropoda (literally 'jointed foot') insects have an external skeleton encasing their internal organs, like a suit of armor. Unlike other arthropods, their body is divided into three parts – head, thorax and abdomen. Insects are the only animals that have three pairs of jointed legs. Most possess wings, which are a sure indicator that an arthropod belongs to the insect class. However most ants are wingless, so absence of wings does not by itself mean that a creature is not an insect.

Left. Wood Ants, are still classified as insects, although they have no wings.

Above. The massive crop damage caused by locusts proves their strength in numbers.

STRENGTH IN NUMBERS

Insects have discovered the basic premise that there is strength in numbers. Their life cycles are quite short, less than one year in most cases and many are much shorter, either by design or through predation. They compensate for this by producing astronomical numbers of offspring; so many in fact, that were it not for the world's insect-eating animals we would surely be overrun within a very short time indeed.

INSECT ADAPTABILITY

High reproductivity and short life spans provide insects' greatest advantage – adaptability. Mutations are random physical, biological or behavioral adaptations which improve and strengthen every population of organisms. When large numbers of offspring are produced quickly, mutations are consequently more frequent, and 'improved' individuals rapidly pass on their advantageous traits, transforming the population.

Insect Wings and Flight

Flight played a large role in the success of insects. They were the first creature on Earth capable of flight, which allowed them to escape their enemies, search out food, water or mates and to colonize new territory.

FIND A SUNNY SPOT

Except for flies, all flying insects have two pairs of wings. It is likely that their wings originated as flaps that could be extended from the thorax allowing wingless insects to escape danger by leaping and gliding away. Insect wings are unique, having evolved specifically for flight, while those of birds are modifications of existing limbs.

EARLY WINGS

The earliest insects known to be capable of true flight had two pairs of wings, that remained extended and did not fold even when resting. Each pair flapped independently of the other pair. This feature can still be seen in the wings of dragonflies, which are members of an insect order that is primitive but common.

Left. The Emperor Dragonfly uses its wings as independent pairs in primitive fashion.

Above. Butterflies coordinate their wings to form two flight surfaces rather than four.

ADVANCED FLIGHT

Many advanced insects, such as the beetles, butterflies and wasps have adapted the anatomy of their wings. They have evolved a method to link the movement of their forewings and hind wings together. This has the effect of allowing the two pairs of wings to operate in tandem, forming two coordinated flight surfaces, rather than four. Most insect wings have distinct patterned veins which help identify each individual species.

PROPULSION

The frequency of wing beats vary from species to species, from one individual to another, and even sometimes in the same individual at different times. In general terms insects such as butterflies which have large, lightweight bodies and large wings need fewer wing beats to stay aloft than insects with small wings and relatively heavy bodies such as a honey-bee. The maximum insect air speed is highly variable between species.

Insect Life Cycles

The vast majority of insects lay eggs. The development of the embryo progresses outside the mother's body. Most species undergo metamorphosis as they mature; There are three different types of metamorphosis: ametabolous, hemimetabolous and holometabolous.

AMETABOLOUS INSECTS

A few primitive insects such as silverfish undergo almost no change between the first nymphal stage and the adult form, except to increase in size. This is known as ametabolous metamorphosis, meaning that there is practically no change in form after the eggs hatch out. The tiny baby silverfish can be seen to be almost exact miniature replicas of the adults.

HEMIMETABOLOUS INSECTS

These insects are characterized by incomplete metamorphosis with immature nymphs that look like adults except in size, wing and sexual organ development. Wings develop with successive skin molts through a series of instar stages, each resembling the adult more closely than the previous one. Molting allows growth, as the newer skin is more elastic.

Left. Silverfish undergo no metamorphosis at all during their life cycle and are known as ametabolous insects.

Above. This group of shield bugs contains one adult with fully developed wings and three nymphs with developing wing buds.

HOLOMETABOLOUS INSECTS

A complete metamorphosis life cycle has four distinct stages. From the egg hatches a larva whose primary function is to eat and grow. Worm-like larvae do not resemble adults; in fact they scarcely resemble insects at all. Larvae molt several times to accommodate their rapidly expanding size at each stage.

At the end of the larval stage a pupa emerges from a final molt. In this stage the great transformation takes place. Inside the pupal case, tissues differentiate, others breakdown and are reabsorbed to form new adult structures like wings. The pupal stage lasts four days to several months, depending on the species, ending with a crumpled soft-bodied adult emerging.

Insect Senses

Humans imagine that all creatures perceive the world in the same way we do, but this is not the case. Many animals see no colors while hearing sounds that are inaudible to us and smelling scents that we cannot.

INSECT VISION

Ultraviolet as a color is invisible to humans, yet insects can see it and respond to it, a fact not lost on flowering plants that depend on insects for pollination. Red, on the other hand, a warm and attractive color to humans, is invisible to insects. Even the colors mutually visible to both insects and humans do not translate into similar images in our respective brains.

INSECT EYES

Insects have compound eyes with several thousand individual ocular lenses. The quality of the image is not known, but these eyes are supremely adapted to detect every movement. Each lens is stimulated separately, with slight movements multiplied many times. The result must be like watching the same channel on hundreds of television sets simultaneously.

Left. The compound eye of the insect has thousands of separate lenses which detect even the slightest movement many times over through each individual ocular cell.

Above. Some flowering plants, dependent on insects such as bees for pollination, attract them by using ultraviolet colors invisible to the human eye.

TASTE, SMELL AND HEARING

The world of insects consists more of patterns of smells and tastes than of light and sound. Taste, smell, touch and hearing are all functions of minute hair-like bristles which cover the body, but they are usually concentrated on the legs, antennae and mouthparts.

Although insects have no noses, their olfactory sense is keener than we can imagine. They smell primarily with their antennae which may also perceive touch, taste and/or sound. Insects can also taste through chemosensory cells on their mouthparts and legs. Sensitivity to sound varies widely among insects. Some simply detect air vibrations with antennae, while others may have more complex structures with vibrating membranes which stimulate phonoreceptor nerves in a similar fashion to the human ear. Insect 'ears', however, are able to detect a much broader range of sound frequencies than the human ear.

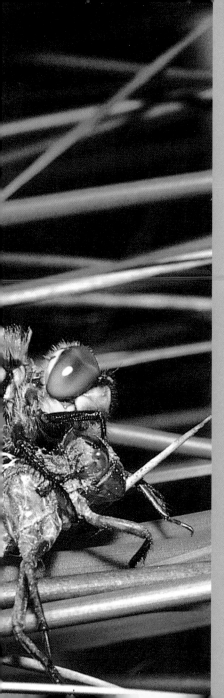

INSECT SPECIES

Key to symbols

The icons used in the directory to describe each insect are explained below.

Insect Order

	Bristletail	Mayfly	
	Dragonfly	Grasshopper	
	Earwig	Cockroach	
	Stick Insect	Bug	
	Lacewing	Beetle	
	Butterfly	Fly	
	Wasp		

Size (in)

Habitat

	Grassy areas scrub & heath	Watersides & riverbanks	
	Woodlands	Ponds & still water	
	Tropical forests	Buildings	

SILVERFISH

A wingless insect, covered in silvery scales, that lives mainly in the dark, damp areas of houses. They are nocturnal and very fast runners, feeding on molds, starchy material and can seriously damage books and papers.

Order Bristletail.
Scientific name *Lepisma saccharina.*
Size 3/8in.
Habitat Mainly in houses and other buildings, but often outdoors.

3/8 in

MAYFLY

There are several similar species, but this insect can be distinguished by its cream or grayish abdomen. They are mainly nocturnal and have three tail filaments. They inhabit areas near lakes and rivers where silt or fine sand is deposited and take two years to become adults.

Order Mayfly.
Scientific name *Ephemera danica.*
Size 1/2in.
Habitat Waterside areas.

1/2 in

BANDED DEMOISELLE

The sexes are different colors: the male has a metallic blue body and the female is metallic green, changing to bronze with age and the wings are yellowish - green. They frequent slow-moving rivers and canals, with muddy deposits.

Order Dragonfly.
Scientific name *Calopteryx splendens.*
Size 1³/₄in.
Habitat Waterside plantlife.

LARGE RED DAMSELFLY

Both sexes have red abdomens with black marks, but the male has less black than the female. They both have red stripes on a black thorax, and the female has a thin black line down the middle of her abdomen.

Order Dragonfly.
Scientific name *Pyrrhosoma nymphula.*
Size 1¹/₂in.
Habitat Waterside areas.

COMMON HAWKER

The abdominal spots on the male are blue and paired; in the female they are yellow or green. There are narrow yellow stripes on top of the thorax in the male, but none in the female. The front of the wings has a bright yellow stripe on each side.

Order Dragonfly.
Scientific name *Aeshna juncea*.
Size 3¹/₈in.
Habitat Open country and watersides, especially those with reedbeds.

GOLD-RINGED DRAGONFLY

The sexes are similar except the male's hindwings are sharply angled and the females are rounded. There are narrow yellow rings on the black abdomen and a small, yellow triangle just behind the eyes.

Order Dragonfly.
Scientific name *Cordulegaster boltonii*.
Size 3¹/₂in.
Habitat Watersides, especially those with fast water.

EMPEROR DRAGONFLY

These are the largest and swiftest of European dragonflies. They are easy to recognize, being the only family of dragonflies whose compound eyes meet along the top of the head. They are also the dragonfly most likely to be some distance from water. The female lays her eggs in submerged plants in weedy pools of water. The adult male has a deep blue, black-lined abdomen and unstriped, greenish thorax. The female has a greenish-blue abdomen. The wings are clear and they are named for their resemblance in flight to hawks.

Order Dragonfly.
Scientific name Anax imperator.
Size $3^3/8$in.
Habitat Waterside plants and open water.

 $3^3/8$ in

BROAD BODIED CHASER

This species breeds in ponds and still water with lots of vegetation. Immature males resemble the female, shown above. The adult male has a powder-blue abdomen with yellow spots. They hunt from a perch to which they return after each hunting session.

Order Dragonfly.
Scientific name *Libellula depressa*.
Size 1³/₄in.
Habitat Watersides areas.

FOUR-SPOTTED CHASER

This species are great migrants, breeding in ponds and lakes. They derive their name from the spot in the centre of the front edge of each wing. The dark patches at the base of the forewing are not always present.

Order Dragonfly.
Scientific name *Libellula quadrimaculata*.
Size 1³/₄in.
Habitat Wet areas such as bogs and heaths and in open country.

CLUB-TAILED DRAGONFLY

This species is recognizable by its abdomen which is black and swollen or clubbed at the end. They have black legs and yellow stripes on the thorax. They breed in slow-moving rivers, though adults can be found far from the water.

Order Dragonfly.
Scientific name *Gomphus vulgatissimus.*
Size $2^1/4$in.
Habitat Waterside areas.

RED SKIMMER

This dragonfly has a brightly colored body with a large wingspan. Males and females can be colored differently. They enjoy perching on plants at quiet streams, lakes and ponds. They move with sgreat speed and are able to hover.

Order Dragonfly.
Scientific name *Libellula saturata.*
Size 3in.
Habitat Watersides, especially those with fast water.

EGYPTIAN GRASSHOPPER

They have vertically striped eyes and a nothched central ridge on the pronotum. They do not sing, fly well, and feed on a variety of shrubs and trees. The hind femur inner surface is pink, the tibia is bluish-gray with white spines. The nymphs are green or orange-brown.

Order Grasshopper.
Scientific name *Anacridium aegyptium.*
Size 1³/4in.
Habitat Coarse planted areas.

  1³/4 in

GREAT GREEN BUSH-CRICKET

This species is recognizable by its size and the brown stripe on the head and thorax. They can fly well, but mostly remain in dense undergrowth eating. Their song is loud and can be heard in late afternoon and evening.

Order Cricket.
Scientific name *Tettigonia viridissima.*
Size 2¹/4in.
Habitat Nettle-beds, shrubs and rough grown areas.

  2¹/4 in

MOLE CRICKET

These crickets are tunnellers with strong front legs. They feed mostly on other animals, but chew roots and damage crops. The forewings are short, but the hindwings are fully developed. They fly on warm evenings.

Order Cricket.
Scientific name *Gryllotalpa gryllotalpa*.
Size 1³/4in.
Habitat Heathland, cultivated land and grassland with damp soil.

WOOD CRICKET

The species illustrated is a female with short, diverging forewings. The male forewings reach halfway along the abdomen. This ground-dweller is flightless and feeds on dead leaves and fungi. They are very nimble and good at leaping. Their song is soft and not easily heard, day or night.

Order Cricket.
Scientific name *Nemobisus sylvestris*.
Size ¹/3in.
Habitat Edges of deciduous woods.

MIGRATORY LOCUST

There are two types solitary and gregarious. European species are of the solitary form, and do little damage to crops. The gregarious form can make huge swarms in Africa. The male makes a harsh sound when courting and is shown here.

Order Grasshopper.
Scientific name *Locusta migratoria.*
Size 1³/₄in.
Habitat Dense vegetation.

AMERICAN COCKROACH

Although originally from Africa, this insect is now found all over the world. They are fast running scavengers, and can be known as the ship cockroach. They fly well in warm conditions.

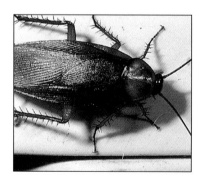

Order Cockroach.
Scientific name *Peroplaneta americana.*
Size 1³/₄in.
Habitat Sewers, mines, greenhouses and warm buildings.

COMMON EARWIG

Easily recognized by the pincers which are long and curved in the male, shown opposite, and slender and almost straight in the female. Both sexes are capable of flying but rarely do so. They are mostly vegetarian.

Order Earwig.
Scientific name *Forficula auricularia.*
Size $^1/_2$in.
Habitat Gardens and houses, almost anywhere.

GIANT OR TAWNY EARWIG

The color of this species of earwing varies from sandy-gray to reddish brown. They burrow in the sand and debris during the daytime and scavenges for food, such as small insects, at night. They rarely fly although they have wings. The male with gently curving pincers is shown opposite.

Order Earwig.
Scientific name *Labidura riparia.*
Size $^7/_8$in.
Habitat Seashores and river banks, rubbish dumps.

PRAYING MANTIS

Mantis are easily recognized by their long slender bodies and slow but graceful movements. They have two pairs of walking legs, and toothed, muscular forelegs that are well adapted to seizing prey at great speed. This pair of front legs are held close to the body in a praying position, hence the name 'praying mantis'. Their heads have an amazing range of movement. They are masters of disguise; often leaf-shaped, they may be brown, pink or green. Lying in wait for their prey, they strike out and eat the prey, dead or alive.

Order Cockroach.
Scientific name *Mantis religiosa.*
Size Up to 3in.
Habitat Rough grassy and bushy areas.

3 in

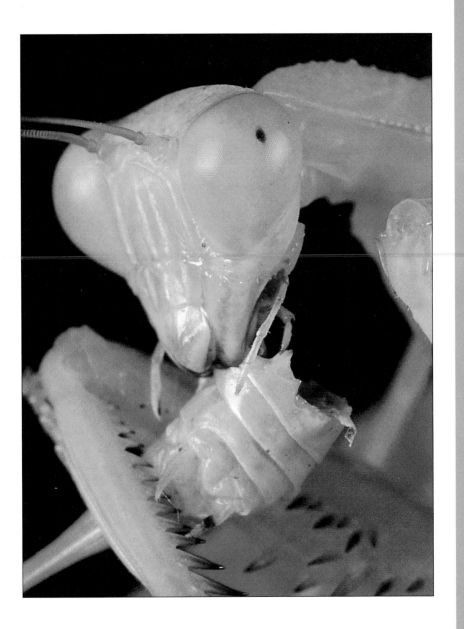

STICK INSECT

Masters of mimicry, stick insects are nearly invisible in their natural habitat. Resembling twigs, they are able to adopt a slow, swaying stride that copies the motion of wind-blown vegetation. Almost all specimens are female, which lay fertile eggs without mating.

Order Stick insect.
Scientific name *Clonopsis gallica.*
Size Up 3^1/2in.
Habitat Hedgerows, gardens and bushy areas.

GIANT SPINY STICK INSECT

First found in 1978 in New Guinea, its habits are unusual: rather than climbing, it spends much of its time on the ground hiding under vegetation. It will consume a wide variety of greens, including grass. Handling needs to be carefully carried out, because these insects are well-protected with a range of spines down the sides of their body.

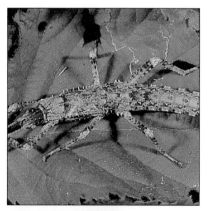

Order Stick insect.
Scientific name *Eurycantha calarata.*
Size 6in.
Habitat Tropical woodland.

JUNGLE NYMPH

The females of this species are truly stunning, but need careful handling because of their long, sharp spines, especially those on the hind legs. They resemble leaves rather than sticks, in view of the width of their body. Males are smaller and brown, females are lime green.

Order Stick insect.
Scientific name *Heteropteryx dilatata*.
Size 7in.
Habitat Tropical woodland.

MADAGASCAN PINK-WINGED STICK INSECT

These slender stick insects are able to fly as a last resort if danger threatens, but they usually keep their wings hidden along their back. Twitching of the legs is an indication they are about to fly. Males resemble females but are smaller in size. This species often replicates parthenogenetically.

Order Stick insect.
Scientific name *Sipyloidea sipylus*.
Size 1/3in.
Habitat Tropical woodland.

HAWTHORN SHIELD BUG

These bugs have a distinctive triangular shape and a green scutellum or shield. The red, triangle shape is formed by the forewings and the rear of the pronotum. Birch Shield Bug is similar but smaller. Juniper Shield Bug has less pointed sides on the pronotum.

Order Bug.
Scientific name *Acanthosoma haemorrhoidale.*
Size 1/2in.
Habitat Deciduous woods and hedge areas.

EURYDEMA DOMINULUS

Looking very like a ladybird with its orange or red ground color, the dark spots are black or metallic green. These insects have membranous wings. The patterns vary. They are common pests of the cabbage family.

Order Bug.
Scientific name *Eurydema dominulus.*
Size 1/3in.
Habitat Waste or cultivated ground.

B U G S

GRAPHOSOMA ITALICUM

This striped, shield bug has bold colors to warn birds, that they taste horrible, few predators try to eat them a second time. They are often found feeding on the carrot family. The top of the shield is a matt surface. In self defense, they can emit an offensive liquid from their thoracic glands.

Order Bug.
Scientific name *Graphosoma italicum.*
Size Up to ¹/3in.
Habitat Roadsides, rough ground.

NEZARA VIRIDULA

The adults are a leaf green color, with a clear membrane at the wing-tip. The thorax has a line of three to five small white dots. The head can be a pale brown alongwith the front of the thorax. The nymphs, shown opposite, are often seen in numbers in the autumn, on potato and pea crops.

Order Bug.
Scientific name *Nezara viridula.*
Size ¹/2in.
Habitat Gardens and highly vegetated areas.

FIRE BUG

Firebugs are frequently sun worshippers and they derive safety in numbers. They can often be found in large swarms, on the ground, in early spring. The forewings are usually short, the head is completely black and there is a round spot on each forewing. They feed on seeds and other insects.

Order Bug.
Scientific name *Pyrrhocoris apterus.*
Size 1/3in.
Habitat Woods and well-vegetated areas.

  1/3 in

LYGAEUS EQUESTRIS

This species can be identified by the red head and the white spots on the membranous wing-tip. They feed on herbaceous plants, on the flowers and developing seeds and fruit and are known to damage cauliflowers.

Order Bug.
Scientific name *Lygaeus equestris.*
Size 3/8in.
Habitat Warm, dry places among rough vegetation.

  3/8 in

RED ASSASSIN BUG

The red and black pattern is variable. They have a narrow head and upturned sides to their abdomen. They feed on a wide range of other insects, including bees. They have a powerful, curved beak and stab their prey before sucking out their juices. They can pierce fingers if roughly handled.

Order Bug.
Scientific name *Rhinocoris iracundus.*
Size 3/5in.
Habitat Tall vegetation such as shrubs, in warm sunny positions.

3/5 in

COMMON POND SKATER

The specimen shown is fully winged but most have short wings or none at all. They utilize surface tension, distributing their weight so they can walk on water. They are seen skimming across the surface of still or slow-moving water looking for prey. The front legs are used to grab other insects from the surface of the water.

Order Bug.
Scientific name *Gerris lacustris.*
Size 3/8in.
Habitat Ponds, ditches and still water.

3/8 in

WATER SCORPION

This bug dose not live up to its name, it is quite harmless. They creep over mud and undergrowth, in shallow water, to catch tadpoles, and small fish with their strong front legs. They rarely fly although they are fully winged. All are poor swimmers and so must remain motionless while awaiting prey.

Order Bug.
Scientific name *Nepa cinerea.*
Size $7/8$in.
Habitat Shallow, still or slow moving water.

$7/8$ in

LESSER WATER BOATMAN

This boatman swims right-way-up unlike most backswimmers who swim on their backs. They prey on aquatic insects, terrestrial insects trapped in the surface skin, and small minnows and tadpoles. Courting males attract their mates by rubbing their front legs against their head to produce a 'song'.

Order Bug.
Scientific name *Sigara dorsalis.*
Size $1/3$in.
Habitat Weedy ponds and slow-moving water.

$1/3$ in

B U G S

COMMON FROGHOPPER

They derive their name from their frog-like appearance. Also known as the spittlebug, for the frothy white masses that the nymphs produce to take refuge in as they feed. The adults are grayish or brownish with a variable pattern and the head is often a paler color.

Order Bug.
Scientific name *Philaenus spumarius.*
Size ¹/₆in.
Habitat Wide range of shrubs and herbaceous plants.

¹/₆ in

RED AND BLACK FROGHOPPER

This bug is closely related to the Common Froghopper even though it is brightly colored. It also feeds on herbaceous plants and a wide variety of trees and shrubs. They leap away when disturbed. The nymphs live on roots, protected by a white mass of solidified froth, produced by their mouths as they eat.

Order Bug.
Scientific name *Ceropis vulnerata.*
Size ³/₈in.
Habitat Scrubby areas and woodland edges.

³/₈ in

B U G S

CICADA

Large, stocky insects best known for the shrill call of the males, audible over a long distance. They have prominent membranous wings, the front pair are twice as long as the hind pair. Females lay their eggs in slits in trees and shrubs. The nymphs can emerge as swarms some years.

Order Bug.
Scientific name *Cicada orni*.
Size Up to 1¹/₂in.
Habitat Anywhere where there are trees, especially pine.

ANT LION

The larvae of this insect live in groups, in sandy soil, where they lie in wait for prey to fall into the pit. They live in dry tropical forests in Madagascar and have large spatula-shapes wings and relatively short antennae. At rest they fold their wings back along their body.

Order Lacewing.
Scientific name *Palpares libelluloides*.
Size 2³/₈in.
Habitat Sand dunes and rough grassy areas with light soil.

NEMOPTERA SINUATA

These are delicate insects with weak, fluttering flight. The larvae are ground-dwelling predators, eating many destructive insects, such as aphids. The patterns and colors of this lacewing often mimic those of butterflies and moths.

Order Lacewing.
Scientific name *Nemoptera sinuata.*
Size 2³/₄in.
Habitat Dry scrubby areas with little vegetation.

2³/4 in

GREEN TIGER BEETLE

Fierce predators, especially upon other insects, they are long-legged insects that run and fly swiftly, using their speed to run down prey. They are colorful, often with an iridescent or metallic sheen. They have prominent sickle-shaped mandibles, crossed in front of the head.

Order Beetle.
Scientific name *Cincindela campestris.*
Size $1/2$in.
Habitat Sandy places, including dunes and heathland.

BOMBARDIER BEETLE

Like the tiger beetles, these also run down prey, but are nocturnal predators. When frightened, it bombards it predators with an irritating and foul-smelling aerosol, which it sprays from its abdomen. They feed on small invertebrates.

Order Beetle.
Scientific name *Brachinus crepitans.*
Size $1/3$in.
Habitat Dry grassy areas, under limestone.

NICROPHORUS INVESTIGATOR

These beetles offer a valuable service breaking up and recycling dead animals and decaying vegetation. They have a solid, front orange band and a rear band with a narrow break. The antennae are orange tipped and the hind tibia are straight.

Order Beetle.
Scientific name *Nicrophorus investigator.*
Size $^7/8$in.
Habitat Anywhere in open areas.

$^7/8$ in

PAEDERUS RUBROTHORACICUS

Distinguishable from other species by the orange or chestnut-colored pronotum. They have slender, ant-like bodies. They get their name from roving over the ground with the tip of their abdomen lifted upwards looking for prey. They eat both living and dead animal matter.

Order Beetle.
Scientific name *Paederus rubrothoracicus.*
Size $^1/6$in.
Habitat Damp areas at the edges of waterways.

$^1/6$ in

STAG BEETLE

The large antler's on the male are over-grown jaws, used for wrestling contests between males when attracting mates. The females have normal jaws. The adults feed on sap oozing from damaged logs and trees. The larvae live in decaying wood.

Order Beetle.
Scientific name *Lucanus cervus.*
Size 2in.
Habitat Woods, parks and old trees.

  2 in

RHINOCEROS BEETLE

The name comes from the curved horn on the male's head. Females have no horn. These are nocturnal scavengers and play an important role in recycling carrion, dung, and decomposing vegetation. The lamellate antennae are tipped with comb-like processors which can be rolled into a ball or unfurled.

Order Beetle.
Scientific name *Oryctes nasicornis.*
Size 1¹/₂in.
Habitat Oak woods and sawmill locations.

  1¹/₂ in

GREAT DIVING BEETLE

These are large aquatic beetles, found in freshwater habitats. They have streamlined oval bodies which are dark green, brown or brownish-black in color. They visit the surface regularly to renew their air supply, which they store as a bubble under the elytra.

Order Beetle.
Scientific name *Dytiscus marginalis*.
Size 1^1/3in.
Habitat Weedy ponds and still water.

1^1/3in

GLOW-WORM

The name comes from the wingless female who produces a greenish light in the evenings to attract a winged male. The females are larger than the males who have dull brown wings. The larvae look like adult females and feed on small snails.

Order Beetle.
Scientific name *Lampyris noctiluca*.
Size ^{2}/3in.
Habitat Grassy places, including road-side verges: mainly on lime.

2/3 in

SEVEN SPOT LADYBIRD

This is a popular garden insect as they are voracious predators upon aphids, scale insects, mealybugs and mites. They are sold as biological control agents by garden supply companies, because they are so effective. Most are red, orange or yellow with black spots. They have a strong-smelling fluid which they exude if they are handled or attacked by predators. The larvae are just as voracious as the adults. They lie dormant overwinter in huge swarms under bark and leaf litter to keep warm.

Order Beetle.
Scientific name *Coccinella 7-punctata*.
Size ¹/3in.
Habitat Almost anywhere.

¹/3 in

CURCULIO ELEPHANS

The snout of the female is almost as long as her body. They use this to bore holes into young acorns and chestnuts where she lays her eggs. The grubs feed inside the developing nuts. The snout on the male is slightly shorter.

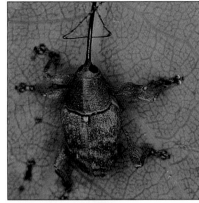

Order Beetle.
Scientific name *Curculio elephans*.
Size 1/3in.
Habitat Oak and chestnut woods.

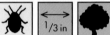

COLORADO BEETLE

Introduced to Europe from America, this beetle is regarded as a pest on potato crops. The adults and grubs feed on the leaves of the potato plants and those of nightshades and other members of the potato family. The colors vary from black and white to yellow and black.

Order Beetle.
Scientific name *Leptinotarsa decemlineata*.
Size 1/3in.
Habitat Farms and gardens.

COCKCHAFER

This beetle flies at night. They have a black pronotum and a pointed abdomen. Also known as the may-bug, the adults eat tree leaves. The grubs eat roots and are considered a serious cereal pest. The antennal club of the male, shown here, opens like a fan and is larger than in the female.

Order Beetle.
Scientific name *Melolontha melolontha.*
Size 1¹/4in.
Habitat Woodland edges, grassland.

CLICK BEETLE

The commonest of the click beetles which uses the clicking noise to startle any predator from attacking it. They are able to repeat the noise several times, if on their backs, and can catapult them-selves right side up, to escape. They are easily recognized by their elongated bullet shape and the large pronotum.

Order Beetle.
Scientific name *Athous haemorrhoidalis.*
Size ¹/2in.
Habitat Woodland areas, hedgerows.

B E E T L E S

SPOTTED LONGHORN BEETLE

The pattern varies and the spots at the front can be faint or absent altogether. The two front pairs of legs are yellow and there are yellow bands on the antennae. The hindwings are usually concealed until just before flight. The adults feed on pollen while the larvae feed on decaying tree stumps.

Order Beetle.
Scientific name *Strangalia maculata.*
Size 2/3in.
Habitat Hedgerows, woodlands and clearings.

OIL BEETLE

Named after the smelly, oily fluids which they emit when frightened. This is the commonest of several flightless beetles. The male is smaller than the female, and has bent antennae. The adults eat plants but the grubs live in the nests of solitary bees. They eat bees and the stored pollen and nectar.

Order Beetle.
Scientific name *Meloe proscarabaeus.*
Size 7/8in.
Habitat Grassy areas.

DANAUS ERESIMNUS MONTEZUMA

The ground color is dusky brown with a black margin, with white speckling, around the wings. The veins are black. This is a migratory butterfly which breeds in Florida.

Order Butterfly.
Common name Soldier.
Size 3^1/8in.
Habitat Grassy areas where the poisonous *Aslepiadacae* grows.

DANAUS PLEXIPPUS

A large and powerful butterfly which has established itself around the world through its great powers of dispersal. Its patterns and colors are not very variable and it has the characteristics of a toxic butterfly. It feeds on milkweed and uses the poisons in the plant for its own defence.

Order Butterfly.
Common name Milkweed, Monarch.
Size 4in.
Habitat Grassy areas where milkweed grows.

COLIAS CROCEUS

One of the most common clouded yellows in Europe, easily recognized by the orange color (not yellow as the common name suggests). It has attractive pink legs and antennae. They visit wild flowers in meadows and along waysides. It is a powerful migrant.

Order Butterfly.
Common name Clouded Yellow.
Size 2^1/4in.
Habitat Meadows, waysides.

2^1/4 in

PALEAOCHRYSOPHANUS HIPPOTHOE

The bright male is suffused with purple around the edges and around the inside hindwing margin. The female has less intense copper and black dots on the forewing with a dark hindwing banded orange. They live in flowery meadows and breed on dock.

Order Butterfly.
Common name Purple-edged Copper.
Size 1^1/2in.
Habitat Flowery meadows.

1^1/2 in

POLYOMNATUS ICARUS

The male has violet-blue uppers and a white fringe. The brown female uppers have a row of marginal orange lunules. Undersides are gray-brown spotted black. The orange spots on the hindwing continue onto the forewing only in the female. They enjoy open sunny locations.

Order Butterfly.
Common name Common Blue.
Size 1^1/3in.
Habitat Sunny areas.

CALYCOPSIS ISOBEON

Dark forewings with orange lines on the undersides. The males have silvery blue on the hindwing. The undersides are beautiful and there is a pair of tails. The butterfly enjoys open areas in secondary forest, and breeds on dead leaves and fruits.

Order Butterfly.
Common name Dusky-blue Hairstreak.
Size ^{3}/4in.
Habitat Secondary forest.

IPHICLIDES PODALIRIUS

This butterfly may be described as 'flying backward' when it glides, as when it flies the long tails and false-eyes are very convincing. It frequents flowery hamlets and breeds on *Prunus* species and fruit trees.

Order Butterfly.
Common name Scarce Swallowtail.
Size 3¹/2in.
Habitat Flowery fields and orchards.

CYNTHIA CARDUI

The most widespread of the world's butterflies and a very powerful migrant. This butterfly is very uniform in its patterns and coloration. Some sub-species do exist. It breeds on a wide variety of plants, including the mallow and daisy families, especially thistles.

Order Butterfly.
Common name Painted Lady.
Size 2³/4in.
Habitat Flowery areas.

HORSE FLY

These flies have amazing compound eyes with iridescent green and purple. The females feed on blood to supply their developing eggs with protein. They fly quietly, unlike mosquitos, and swiftly landing softly before inflicting a painful bite. They also have a prominent spur on their third antennal segment.

Order Fly.
Scientific name *Tabanus sudeticus.*
Size $7/8$in.
Habitat Damp pastures near woods.

ST MARK'S FLY

Named after St Mark's Day (25 April) when huge swarms of these black flies descend over shrubs in spring. Their legs dangle loosely making them look hazardous, but they are harmless. They breed in rotting vegetation and in soil. The larvae feed on plant roots whilst the adults feed on rotting material.

Order Fly.
Scientific name *Bibio marci.*
Size $1/2$in.
Habitat Rough grassy areas, hedgerows, scrub and woodlands.

FLESH FLY

One of a group of flies with very large feet and red eyes. The adults feed on flowers but are attracted to carrion and dung. The female give birth to larvae, not laying eggs, in either dung or carrion. The larvae feed in the rotting material.

Order Fly.
Scientific name *Sarcophaga carnaria.*
Size 2/3in.
Habitat Around houses but almost anywhere.

DRONE FLY

Derives its name from its resemblance to the male Honey bee. They enjoy warm sunny days when they dart and hover, feeding on the nectar. They have a broad, dark stripe on their face and have hairs on the hind legs. The larva lives in stagnant water. They do not sting or bite.

Order Fly.
Scientific name *Eristalis tenax.*
Size 1/2in.
Habitat All areas with flowers.

CRANE FLY

One of the biggest flies in Europe, this species is identified by its wing pattern. The male has a blunt abdomen whilst the female has a pointed abdomen. The larvae live in mud at the edges of streams and ponds. They rest with their wings wide apart, never folding them over their body.

Order Fly.
Scientific name *Tipula maxima.*
Size 1¹/4in.
Habitat Riversides, marshes and damp woodland.

BEE FLY

These are easy to identify as they have a long proboscis, used to probe flowers for nectar. The sound that this fly makes, resembles that of a bee, and they are often mistaken for bees. They are harmless and furry with a bold brown wing pattern. The grubs are dropped as larvae to develop in the nests of solitary bees and wasps.

Order Fly.
Scientific name *Bombylius major.*
Size ³/8in.
Habitat Sunny locations in woods and clearings, roadsides and fields.

DUNG FLY

These flies swarm on fresh dung and often mate while at least one is still feeding. Eggs are deposited in the dung, and the larvae develop rapidly. the female is less hairy and greenish. The males are golden-haired, but both sexes have black antennae. Adults feed on flies attracted to the dung, while the larvae feed on the dung itself.

Order Fly.
Scientific name *Scathophaga stercoraria.*
Size ¹/3in.
Habitat Woodlands, pastures.

ROBBER FLY

These are predatory flies which often prey upon resting insects larger than themselves, attacking from above and using stout mouthparts. pierce the victim and drain out the body fluids. They mimic damselflies and bumble-bees. They have bristles to protect their eyes from attack by their victims.

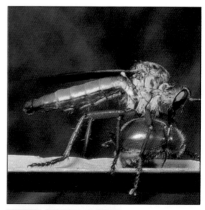

Order Fly.
Scientific name *Asilus carbroniformis.*
Size 1¹/4in.
Habitat Open areas where dung is deposited.

MASON WASP

A solitary wasp, sometimes known as the wall mason wasp, as it makes its nest with mud or clay in crevices. Difficult to identify as most of the distinguishing features are located on the underside. They usually have a square mark at the front of the abdomen.

Order Wasp.
Scientific name *Ancistrocerus nigricornis.*
Size 3/8in.
Habitat Trees, rocks, and walls where it can nest, often around houses.

GREATER HORN TAIL

These sawflies can look formidable but they are harmless. The females have a saw-like ovipositor and use it to insert eggs into plant tissue. At the same time they inject a substance which shelters and provides food for the larva. The grubs feed on the timber. Also known as the wood wasp.

Order Wasp.
Scientific name *Urocerus gigas.*
Size 2in.
Habitat Woodland and sawmill timber.

PAPER WASP

So called as they live in colonies where the nest is made of wood fibre. The nests are not very large and are found on buildings, in stone walls and occasionally in vegetation. They can inflict painful stings, and alarm pheromones released by disturbed individuals can incite group attacks.

Order Wasp.
Scientific name *Polistes gallicus*.
Size ¹/2in.
Habitat Anywhere except dense woodland.

ICHNEUMON WASP

These are parasitic wasps with a red band, yellow or cream scutellum and cream spots at the rear of the abdomen. The larvae are major parasites, attacking larvae of many beetles and of their own order. The eggs are laid in caterpillars, especially those of the swift moth.

Order Wasp.
Scientific name *Ichneumon suspiciosus*.
Size ¹/2in.
Habitat Hedgerows and grassy areas.

DELTA UNGUICULATA

These are solitary wasps which construct their nests by making a ball of sand and clay. These balls are then hung on a ceiling or overhang, and each is furnished with food, usually small caterpillars and an egg.

Order Wasp.
Scientific name *Delta unguiculata.*
Size 7/8in.
Habitat Often near water, around houses.

HORNET

These wasps nest in hollow trees and cavities, feeding the grubs on insects and butterflies. They are colonial, laying their eggs in cells made of a paper substance. As adults, they are less aggressive than other wasps. They are recognized by their brown and gold pattern and deeply notched eyes.

Order Wasp.
Scientific name *Vespa crabro.*
Size 1 1/3in.
Habitat Tree planted areas, including gardens.

WHITE TAILED BUMBLE BEE

These are social bees as opposed to solitary bees. They live in colonies with queens, males and workers. They have a lemon-yellow collar and the white tail identifies this species.

Order Wasp.
Scientific name *Bombus lucorum.*
Size 2/3in.
Habitat Nests in the ground and can be found anywhere.

HONEY BEE

This is the bee that provides our honey and most live in hives, although some do live in wild colonies. They have a long, narrow cell near the wing-tip which distinguishes it from other bees.

Order Wasp.
Scientific name *Apis mellifera.*
Size 1/2in.
Habitat All flowered areas.

WOOL CARDER BEE

This bee can be found on plants with wooly leaves. The hairs are gathered by the female who rolls them into a ball. These are then used to line her nest in a hole in wood or masonry. They have yellow or orange spots on the sides of their abdomen. The thorax is black.

Order Wasp.
Scientific name *Anthidium manicatum.*
Size $^1/_2$in.
Habitat Woodland areas, parks gardens, hedgerows.

 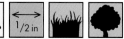

1/2 in

LEAF CUTTER BEE

This bee cuts into rose leaves in gardens leaving oval and semicircular holes behind. The leaf pieces are used to make cells for the grubs.

Order Wasp.
Scientific name *Megachile centuncularis.*
Size $1/3$in.
Habitat Woodlands, gardens and hedgerows.

TAWNY MINING BEE

Named after its abdomen and mining activities in the ground. Once it hatches from its subterranean cell during the winter, the bee comes to the surface and flies off in the spring. Some live in colonies, where the number of nests can be a thousand or more.

Order Wasp.
Scientific name *Andrena fulva.*
Size $3/8$in.
Habitat Woodlands, gardens and hedgerows.

CARPENTER BEE

These are common bees and visit flowers such as wisteria. They fill in holes in buildings and walls with pollen and lay eggs on top of that. A large bee with a shiny black body and wings that reflect blue and violet. They can be alarming as their flight is noisy but they rarely sting and are not aggressive.

Order Wasp.
Scientific name *Xylocopa violacea.*
Size 1^1/4in.
Habitat Flowery areas and gardens.

  1^1/4 in

WOOD ANTS

One of a group of mound-building ants. They have a black head and abdomen, and a reddish-brown thorax. They do not sting but fire formic acid from the rear when frightened. They feed mainly on other insects.

Order Wasp.
Scientific name *Formica rufa.*
Size ^{3}/8in.
Habitat Woodlands.

  ^{3}/8 in

W A S P S

Index

INDEX